Do Listen

Understand what's really being said.
Find a new way forward

Bobette Buster

Published by
The Do Book Company 2018
Works in Progress Publishing Ltd
thedobook.co

A CIP catalogue record for this book
is available from the British Library

ISBN 978-1-907974-52-6

10 9 8 7 6 5 4 3 2

To find out more about our company,
books and authors, please visit
thedobook.co or follow us **@dobookco**

5% of our proceeds from the sale of
this book is given to The Do Lectures
to help it achieve its aim of making
positive change **thedolectures.com**

Cover designed by James Victore
Book designed and set by Ratiotype

Printed and bound by OZGraf Print
on Munken, an FSC-certified paper

MIX
Paper from
responsible sources
FSC® C163799

To my mother, Shirley.

The greatest listener I have ever known.
Quiet, non-judgmental, ever kind,
she was always available to listen.
And she did it so well, always creating
a common good in her everyday life.
As my father said, shortly before he
passed, 'I never heard an unkind word
said about her.'

Contents

No story lives
unless someone
wants to listen

—

J.K. Rowling

Prologue

As a child, I was insatiably curious. The storytelling in my small world was wondrous, and I was always delighted to listen. I didn't want to miss a thing. I'd be sent to bed, or out of the room, but then I'd tiptoe back down the stairs to listen at the crack of the door. My mother would find me asleep at the bottom of the staircase.

Or I would crawl under my grandmother's grand dining table and curl up into a ball so no one would know I was there. Then I'd experience 360 degrees of true surround sound. I heard the hilarity and the poetic, ironic quips of my family – their grace with language, witty asides, rhythmic cadences. All this rang out above and around me.

Introduction

You cannot truly listen to anyone
and do anything else at the same time.

—

M. Scott Peck, *The Road Less Travelled*

Over the past 25 years, I've listened to well over 10,000 stories as a film production executive and story consultant, and while also lecturing in film school courses and facilitating storytelling workshops all over the world. When I first began this career, my intention was simply to listen to each story. Did the narrative work? How could it be improved? I had to learn the right questions to ask of both the story and the storyteller. But over time, I began to observe that when I was listening to the best stories – most often in a workshop setting – there was something deeper going on.

The storyteller possesses a powerful need – an *urge* – to tell their story. It's personal to them. And there is often a point in a well-told story, when everyone in the room – including me – leans in. We quietly give the storyteller all the time they need to tell the full tale. We're actively listening.

As their story shifts, the room shifts. We are all ears, listening with full attention, as if gathered around a campfire. A bond develops. As the story comes to a close, inexorably, we are changed – as the story has indeed changed the storyteller. And, in the end, our listening resonates in palpable heartfelt connections. And, yes, it's emotional: tears, outbursts of laughter, smiles. People reach out to each other. And invariably they say, 'Wow.' They usually have no adequate words for the experience.

In one such group of about fifteen entrepreneurs – leaders in their fields, each successful in their own right – I gathered everyone round a table, effectively creating a story circle. I began by asking one simple question: 'Tell us something about yourself that we would otherwise never know.' Their answers vary widely, of course, and some are very personal. But, I tell them, this is not therapy. I am mostly there to curate the time, so that everyone in the group has a chance to share. I monitor the experience carefully.

The first couple of stories are usually not very substantive as, of course, the participants do not want to embarrass themselves. But invariably, over the course of the session, they share a story that becomes profound. I've never known this *not* to happen. Why? Because I think people long to tell their story, and they just haven't had the right opportunity to be *heard*. But it's only in the process of the telling, that they discover why the story matters to them.

To give you an example, the following story experience has long resonated with me.

Tom was a trim, physically fit man in his fifties, dressed in jeans with a smart shirt and sweater. An upper-level executive, he had spent more than twenty years at a major communications company. He was attending the workshop with several colleagues.

On this day, Tom was the third one to speak. True to form, after the first two participants shared incidental personal stories, Tom spoke freely when it was his turn. He said that he had left home young, around fourteen years old, and led a peripatetic life. He earned enough money through odd jobs to party each weekend, which usually meant getting stoned or drunk with his friends. This went on for years until early one Monday morning, when he was 29, Tom woke up in a diner booth, and realised he'd been on a four-day bender. He couldn't even remember what had happened. Total blackout. It was then that he decided he was done with drinking. He didn't want this life any more. Tom ended his story there. Job done, he assumed his turn was over. He had answered the exercise objective: he had told a story out loud that we would otherwise never have known.

The room was poleaxed. We did not expect this story from the healthy-looking, successful man in our midst. But I knew there was more to be heard. So rather than moving on to the next person, I simply asked, 'What time of day was it, when you woke up?' He reflected, 'Around ten in the morning.'

I continued, 'What did you see?'

'I remember there was this godawful floor polisher cleaning the floor, all around me. Just a terrible drone. And there was that sick-sweet smell of cleaning – all the tables and plastic booths – going on all around me. And they'd opened the windows; the morning light was knifing through. They were cleaning all around me. Who knows how long I'd been there?'

'What did you do next?'

'I went outside in the bright light and found a phone booth. That was when they had those Yellow Pages hanging in a thick book. I found the number for Alcoholics Anonymous. Someone answered. All I remember is that they took down my address, said I should go home, and they would send someone over for me that day to take me to a meeting.'

'And what did you do when you got home?'

'I tore through my house and found every bottle – and poured out all the contents. Wherever they were stashed, under the sink, wherever. I flushed them all down the toilet. And then I sat down and waited.'

'And … did someone come?'

'Yes, I remember sitting by the radiator watching the sun go down, waiting until about five.'

'That was a long time to wait, wasn't it?'

'I don't remember. I was just so grateful they had promised a person would show up that day.'

'And …?'

'They did. They took me to my first meeting.'

'And … now, twenty years on?'

'I never had another drink after that day.'

Silence enveloped the room. Or, I should say, *listening*. Everyone's emotions were pent up to bursting. We were all tuned in to Tom. Why? Because he was so open – and vulnerable. How had this story of a young man who spoke of cleaning products, phone booths and waiting by a radiator captured their attention?

Because there was another story quietly sitting behind the first one. I knew that if he could simply make us see the world as he saw it that day – in all its boring, prosaic details – that we would be there with him. The true story would reveal itself. So I asked: 'How was it that you'd spent almost half your life – from the age of 14 to age 29 – without any apparent direction or training for a better job, and you'd become an alcoholic? What are the odds that someone like that would pick themselves up and choose to change? What made this day of all days different?'

Tom looked away, and said, 'I don't know why I told this story today. You know, I've never told anyone this story.' His fellow colleagues nodded in astonishment. 'I don't know why I did today.'

But I knew it was because Tom *needed* to tell the story of the moment when he took control of his life. *Carpe diem*. When he discovered his own courage. Young 29-year-old Tom, who had spent half his life 'locked out of his brain', had made a simple clear-cut choice to do something he'd never done before. He acknowledged he needed help, and let go. This was an act of great bravery.

Why did he tell this story, in full, on this day? Because I simply listened and asked active memory questions that appealed to the senses. Ordinary ones. What did you see? What time of day was it? What did you hear? What did you do next? Ordinary details – cleaning smells, floor-buffer drone, the Yellow Pages, flushing a toilet, sitting by a radiator – all this, the dull stuff of life, make us all connect. And in the ordinary, we can now expect the extraordinary to happen.

These are Sense Memories. I asked the group afterwards, 'What one detail first comes to mind, when you remember Tom's story?' Most said the Yellow Pages, or the bright morning sun and how he sat until the sunset and the AA friend arrived. The colour yellow encompassed them all. I call this the Gleaming Detail – because in that one detail, the entire story comes alive.

I asked the group what they responded to, even though I knew their answers would come down to the moment of Tom's active choice. When he found the Yellow Pages, he was choosing to find help. And he did. Tom was revealing a moment of profound personal courage. The thing about sharing a personal story about courage is this: If I can visualise your act of courage, I am emboldened to discover my own courage, too. Just as Tom needed to tell his story, *we* needed to hear it. Courage is a spiritual muscle that, once activated, can stimulate the imaginations of other people and inspire them to make their own choices, too.

We open our hearts to wonder. If we can hear and see it, we can be it. We can do it, too. And in this book we'll hear more about how the act of listening can ennoble others and be a catalyst for change.

From then on, the class blossomed into a full day of the participants sharing moments of fear and cowardice overcome, hilarious breakthroughs, or quiet revelation. By the end of the day, the group had bonded, and many had developed friendships that carry forward to this day. This is not an uncommon outcome from my sessions.

In the case of Tom's story, we listened to a man take up the courage one dreary Monday morning to grab hold of his life and never look back. We became strengthened and emboldened, just by the act of listening. In listening, we gave Tom the permission and space to speak aloud about what had been a closed part of his life. Imagine if we did this for other people we meet? What if each of us took the time to listen to just one other person in this way? And it doesn't have to be a stranger: what about our nearest and dearest?

> There is no greater agony than bearing an untold story in you.
>
> Maya Angelou

Over time, I came to see that the act of listening had a transformative effect on anyone in the room. I could 'hear' the shift and feel the palpable connection – or, by contrast, the lack of interest when people stopped listening, the energy seeming to drain from the room like a balloon seeping air. As I tuned in to these experiences, I developed a kind of radar to feel the power of the story or to read the mood of a room – and I began to observe how I could orchestrate it for the better. All by listening.

The hidden world reveals itself when we listen.

This book is about rediscovering the lost art of listening, and then using that ability to form deeper connections and generate moments of wonder. Once you listen well to another person, you both connect. You are never the same again. We break through our own limitations and self-interest. Listening is the only way we can continue to grow and flourish as individuals – and as a society.

My Process

All of us are living a story. And behind this, we have an untold story that we long to tell. But sometimes we don't yet know it, or know how to make ourselves heard.

Here are some pointers on how I have learned to listen and draw out these untold stories in my workshops, classes, and daily life.

My process is this: I take the time necessary, and I ask simple questions, to open up a common space between us, such as:

— 'What happened next?'

— 'What time of day was it?' 'Where were you?'
   'What do you remember from that moment?'

— 'Why do you think you did that?'

These kinds of questions always elicit vivid memories and energise the storyteller's passion for the story.

Then at the appropriate moment, I pause.

I acknowledge the storyteller's moment of courage – that moment when they made a significant change in their life – because *that* moment is inevitably why they have chosen to tell this story, though they typically didn't realise that was why, not at first.

As the storyteller becomes more relaxed, I embolden them by asking the following:

— 'How did you feel?' (Normally, they can't answer the 'feeling' question too well.)

— 'How do you feel now?'

Often they are deeply moved – because in your listening to them, you have brought them out into a wider, more open space.

They have felt *heard*. There is great power is this act. A new trust has been born.

And if you are in a group setting, you will most certainly experience the unleashed desire for everyone else to want to be heard, too.

We have forgotten
the power of silence

1
The Lost Art of Listening

Why is it we feel surprised, even grateful, when someone really hears us – when someone leans in and gives us their time and attention? How has this basic act and most primal of senses become such a rare commodity in today's world? Has the one-way street of social media 'broadcasting' really marked the end of conversation and listening?

A US national news channel recently conducted an experiment with a small group of teenagers between fourteen and sixteen years old – the generation sometimes known as screenagers. The reporter's story was addressing the latest scientific studies that suggest smartphones encourage addictive behaviours, encourage ADHD, depression, FOMO (fear of missing out), and so on. Her experiment was to see what would happen if she took away the teenagers' smartphones and laptops. They were to go cold turkey for one full week.

I expected that the teens would report great resentment, high anxiety, and frustration at being cut off. And, of course, some of them did. But they also knew this experiment had an end date, which likely mitigated some of those negative feelings. When they were asked how they felt at the end of the week, to the reporter's – and my own – surprise, all of the students responded with what I call 'curious wonder'. They were slightly amazed at how much they enjoyed talking with their families over dinner. They found time for conversation with their friends. They got their homework done, finished their chores – much to their parents' amazement. It is often said that the smartphone has killed small talk as well as the quiet ability to just hang out and learn to handle boredom. When the teens were asked what they took away from this week-long famine of social media connectivity, one fifteen-year-old girl said, 'I really want to stop using my phone, and learn to just *be* with my friends.' Face to face. Not in a group with each person's face pressed into their individual screens. She was genuinely filled with a curious hope. Like she'd never encountered this thought before. What a novel idea!

It's interesting to note that when each of us was in our mother's womb, our eyes were closed but our ears already worked. We heard her heartbeat, the swishing of the amniotic fluid, the jolt of loud noises in the outer world. That was our world. As such, our hearing is connected to our primal emotions and memories. Only when we are born do our eyes open, gather focus, and take in all the light and tonal differences of this new world. Since our eyes are on the front of our face, our main reference point from then on is visual – our perspective is usually based on whatever our eyes can see. Listening retreats to the periphery, a dancing shadow, insofar as our perception is concerned. But it remains the ambient light of our emotions, hard-wired to our first feelings. From the time our ears are formed, they remain on, 24/7. Our hearing is our last sense to go when we die. This is why the Greeks said that our ears are the 'guardian of our sleep'. A mother will hear her baby cry in the dead of night.

Medical science has discovered that the minute hair fibres lining the cochlea in our ear canal contract and expand, similar to the irises of our eyes. They do so in response to sound waves coming in. Our ears are alerting and protecting us as best they can, but ever since the Industrial Age, our ears have been under assault. Now, we close our ears to all the overlapping, nonstop sonic intrusions. We are selective – choosing to block out the natural world with our headphones, empowered to choose what we want to hear. But in doing so, we are no longer able to sense what is calling us. We have lost the ability to listen. We have forgotten – if we ever knew – the power of silence. We cannot remember how the birds and animals speak – and why we even need to know what they are saying.

Before the Industrial Age – roughly the years between the mid-eighteenth and early-twentieth centuries – all humanity existed in a world filled with pastoral, natural sounds. In some cases, sound had a direct bearing on a family's livelihood, as in the case of sheep farmers who relied on the superior hearing of dogs to extend their own honed senses and keep their flock safe from predators.

In the towns, the community news came from the sudden pealing of church bells ringing out from the tallest spire in the town centre, gathering all together as one within its sonic range. The news was sometimes uplifting, sometimes sombre. One would know which by the cadence of the bells' peal. (This tradition continued past the Industrial Age. When President John F. Kennedy was assassinated on 22 November 1963, Queen Elizabeth ordered that the bells of Westminster Abbey be soberly rung once every minute from 11am to noon in the following days – a solemn honour that had historically been reserved only for members of the Royal Family. When reminded of this fact, she simply commanded that the tolling of the Westminster bells be done. And it was.)

In London, there is a small, unique museum called Dennis Severs' House that functions as a 'living experience museum' meant to authentically replicate life in the eighteenth century. In the late twentieth century, Dennis Severs restored a five-storey, ten-room brick home built near Spitalfields Market, not far from the River Thames, and recreated the living conditions of an eighteenth-century middle-class silk merchant as if he were living there with his family and servants. When you walk through the doors, it is like entering the past. There is no electricity or plumbing. The house has been staged as if the family has just been called away. Beside the front entrance, in the parlour, the patriarch's great boots rest by the fire, which is real and glowing. His half-drunk glass of sherry awaits his imminent return. In the cellar, another real fire is lit, ready for the cook's fresh eggs and pastry dough rolled out for baking. The smells entice you, and everything is enhanced by the warmth of the kitchen. Each floor gives you a different window into the experience of daily life in those times. I happened to attend near dusk, and as the interior became progressively darker, I felt the need for a candle even though the weak gas lighting was turned up.

In the attic, where the servants lived – and all of them slept in one bed – there was a feeble fireplace. Beside it was a small child's stool with a tiny cane, as if Tiny Tim himself had just departed. On this particular floor, the museum has unseen speakers that suddenly broadcast the faint bellows of cannon blast, as if the sound were coming off a barge floating down the nearby River Thames. I learned later that the cannon was used in that way to announce important news – in this case that King William IV had just died.

How else would you have known this breaking news? Of course, there would have been the town crier, bellowing 'Hear ye! Hear ye!' and carrying a sign with the headlines. And in later years, the newsboy would holler, 'Read all about it!' as he sold his newspapers to passers-by.

Nearby Hyde Park is famous for its Speakers' Corner, where on occasion people have gathered in their thousands to hear vociferous debate. The American Revolution was fuelled by debates throughout the coffee houses and on the village greens of the thirteen colonies. John Wesley and others who possessed great, booming, stentorian voices led the Great Awakening of evangelicals in Britain. They were able to command the attention of thousands of new converts at that time, while they preached in the great outdoors.

As the Industrial Age fell upon our modern world, our methods of communication changed, and so too did our ability to both hear and listen to sounds in our everyday lives. When I think about the transformation of the sonic landscape, I'm reminded of a story I heard from a fellow film industry professional talking about the challenge of recreating the audio atmosphere of World War One. Gary Rydstrom, an Academy Award-winning sound designer, was working on a 2011 film adaptation of the play (based on the novel), *War Horse*. He wanted to create the aesthetic 'sound shock' of tanks barrelling through the pastoral countryside in France. The developed world was at that time experiencing a quantum leap from horses and mules, to the sonic onslaught of the Industrial Age. The sound of the huge tanks bursting in and crushing fields and crops needed to feel too loud in the film, as it would have felt to the virgin ears of the early twentieth-century villagers: threatening, confusing and disorienting. Successful sound design would make the modern cinema audience experience what those people had felt. And in feeling what they felt, by hearing what they heard, they might understand them better, too.

It is impossible for us to grasp how quiet the world once was. When Alexander Graham Bell invented the telephone, people picked up the ringing line and just listened – in silence. Thus, he also had to decide on a word that could be used so that the person picking up could let the caller know they were on the line – he suggested 'ahoy', but it failed to catch on, and the alternative 'hello' proposed by his rival Thomas Edison soon became widespread. Similarly, when radio communications first came in during World War One, the people on either end of a conversation soon realised that they needed to confirm they were listening – often by saying 'Roger' or 'Roger that' periodically. Otherwise, the speaker might worry they were talking into a silent void.

When the French pilots during the Great War were in trouble they would shout into the radio, *'M'aider! M'aider!'* – a shortened form of *'Venez m'aider'*, French for 'Help me!' This became the international call sign 'Mayday!' for help in a crisis.

As industrialisation became the driving force of modern society, the world became arguably more aggressive and overbearing in its power. As we know, it also brought people by the millions out of the countryside into the cities. So too exploded the rate of loneliness, disconnection, depression and dislocation. In short, the gentle pace and harmony of pastoral life became a thing of the past. Another way to look at it is that the world became less kind.

Over the generations since the industrial revolution changed life as we know it, how have we tamed our noisy, cacophonous world? The government appropriates taxpayers' money to build noise barriers on highways, among other attempts to reduce noise pollution. Businesses hire sound engineers to design quieter offices, and we shelter within our own sonic silos – inside our cars, at home with multiple soundscapes competing for our attention (television, radio, music, and so on). Staring into our screens – though they may be silent – our minds are listening to what's being broadcast to us in steady, unending streams. The ubiquitous smartphone has become the great killer of small talk – the universal way we have connected since time immemorial. Equally ubiquitous today are the earbuds that cocoon us within our own private worlds. No one needs to listen to anything other than what they want to hear any more.

In fact, we are consciously choosing to *not* listen, though the world is crying out to us to pay attention. What would happen if we did that?

He who has ears to hear, let him hear.

Matthew 11:15

Exercise: Consciously tune in to the world

The universe – the sun, stars and wind – conspires to slow us down, to pause, to take a breath, and in doing so, gradually we find ourselves stilled into a state of gratitude for being alive. Even just for a moment. Our ears can help us do this. Here's a short exercise to tune in to the power of listening:

Go for a walk in an urban park, along the shoreline of a beach or stroll down a leafy street where you will undoubtedly hear the chorus of birds, or the leaves rustling. Take time for nature and tune in to your surroundings.

I often ponder the physics of all the waveforms that surround us – thinking about how sound waves travel slower than light. What we *hear* strikes us at a slower rate than what we *see*, which is instantaneous. It's my belief that when we listen – when we consciously tune in to the sounds coming to our attention – this somehow recalibrates our brainwaves, and realigns our hearts and minds. We are stilled. Perhaps this is why we find ourselves in awe when we stop to look at the moon, the sunrise, or the surf rolling onto a beach.

While you're on your walk, take the time to rediscover all those sounds from the natural world seeking you out to grab your attention. Then note how you feel on your return. Perhaps time has somehow expanded around you. And maybe your state of mind, the people you encounter, and the rest of your day will be better for it.

Part of doing
something is listening.
We are listening.
To the sun.
To the stars.
To the wind.

Madeleine L'Engle, *A Swiftly Tilting Planet*

The hidden world
reveals itself
when we listen

2
Sound Memories

Before the invention of the phonograph in 1877, sound was considered the most ephemeral of all the senses. Sounds passed by you, like a waft of perfume. Sound was fleeting. Uncapturable. But when, at last, Thomas Edison captured 'Mary had a little lamb' on his phonograph cylinder, the world was captivated. And it was never the same again. At the end of his life, Edison, who was partially deaf, was asked which one, of over a thousand inventions, was his favourite. Without hesitation he answered, 'Sound recording.'

Sound has the remarkable power to evoke memories and emotional reactions at a primal level. In my work as a film professor, I can't help but reference the quantum leap in cinema sound design since the 1970s. The directors of now-classic films including *A Clockwork Orange* (Stanley Kubrick), *A Star Is Born* (Frank Pierson), *Close Encounters of the Third Kind* (Steven Spielberg) and *The Elephant Man* (David Lynch) all sought to make sound a central part of the cinematic experience. The art form of including sound in movies had been coming into existence since 1927, when Al Jolson first exclaimed off the cuff, 'Wait a minute, you ain't heard nothin' yet!' during *The Jazz Singer*, and from that day on, audiences the world over could not get enough of the 'talkies'.

But it took the cinema of the 1970s to launch the next revolution in sound – which became known as sound design. From Walter Murch's John Cage-inspired sound design for Francis Ford Coppola's *Godfather* trilogy to Ben Burtt's genius creation of George Lucas's *Star Wars* 'sound characters' R2-D2, Chewbacca and Darth Vader, culminating in Walter Murch's innovative surround soundtrack for Coppola's *Apocalypse Now* – these films set the gold standard we all enjoy today.

As the technology advanced, and the theatre-listening experience vastly improved, sound designers were driven to experiment with how best to orchestrate emotions from sound. This could be via the long-distance whistle of a train rumbling towards you (this is always the sound of intractable destiny), a lone dog barking far off (the classic sound of loneliness), or more complex creations such as the ending of *Saving Private Ryan*, for which Gary Rydstrom had to create the feeling of random terror. A small band of American soldiers wait in a bombed-out French village for the dreaded arrival of the Nazis in their much-feared panzer tanks. They never actually see the tanks, but boy do they – and we – hear them. The awesome, ungodly sound of scream-like screeches from the ungreased ball bearings on the tank treads echoes off the town's walls, bringing 'the monster' ever closer, louder and louder. The enemy sounds far bigger than it could be – in 3D, coming from all around them. How many of us could survive the suspense? Through sound, director Steven Spielberg and sound designer Rydstrom capture the fear and bravery of the young men caught in life-and-death combat, and the randomness of war.

When working out how best to tell a story with sound, cinema sound designers ask a lot of questions. What is the story? What is the emotional subtext of this scene? What is the power that sound can bring to the viewer's overall experience of the story? How can sound best connect to the audience as they watch and listen?

Recently, I wrote and produced a feature documentary on the power of sound and storytelling entitled *Making Waves: The Art of Cinematic Sound*. We cover many of the topics mentioned above, but we also asked each of our interviewees to name their favourite childhood sound memory. We were fortunate to interview David Lynch, who replied: 'Whenever I hear the western meadowlark, it takes me right back to my grandfather's ranch which I loved when I was a child.' Walter Murch told of growing up and living within hearing distance of the Carillon Bell Clock Tower in Manhattan. The clock rang out a musical motif every fifteen minutes, then rang the respective number of tolls for each hour (one to twelve, even at midnight). He sang for us the different riffs of those quarter-hour chimes.

One of my African-American colleagues, who would prefer to remain nameless, volunteered their own experience, 'I can tell you my worst childhood sound memory. When I was five, I remember waking up to the sound of my parents shouting. When I looked out of my bedroom window onto our front lawn, I saw a huge burning cross, blazing bright. I learned later that it had been put there by the KKK. But what I remember most is the sound of my parents – their fear – and the crackling fire.'

For me, the exercise took me back to those hot, humid summer nights at the home of my grandmother. I would be out playing with my brother, and when dusk fell, we would be called back inside. At the time, all the houses in the small Kentucky town of Leitchfield had screen doors. As I ran past, I could hear through those screens the televisions playing inside – the canned laughter of a beloved sitcom or the *whack!* of a baseball bat from a National League game and the roar of the crowd. As the mothers called their children in, their screen doors screeched open. And then, as we bounded inside beneath the bright overhead fluorescent kitchen lights, the screen doors would be left to lurch their way back to closed – swinging, creaking and then slamming – *thwack!* It was the sound that we were all in now, safe and sound. By the time I was grown up enough to leave home, everyone had air conditioning, and those evenings of swinging screen doors became a thing of the past. I remember missing that most of all – as a sound of such transparency into other people's homes, welcome realms of warm light in the dark night, and slow swinging doors seeking the latch.

Sound continued to be a touchstone to memory in my life. My brother Charles was a classically trained singer and ended up moving to London and becoming the lead singer in his own pop band. He had big dreams. Sadly both he and his partner fell ill from AIDS and his partner passed away. When Charles's health began to fail, I flew to London to care for him. He died at Middlesex Hospital, aged 29, on 21 March, the first day of spring. One of the details that sticks with me about that day is the quiet all around me. A heavy snow flew into the heart of London – so rare – icing the vibrant daffodils and purple hyacinths. A caked silence stilled the air. Something opened my ears that day. I couldn't sleep for days, not wanting to give in to the dark, and I would wait up for the dawn chorus. It was my one delight.

Some years later, my grandmother passed on at the age of 94, and my mother and I faced the overwhelming task of selling all her things. Her basement was filled with all the flotsam and jetsam of nearly a century of life. There were all iterations of electronica from the 1940s onwards – phones, typewriters, kitchen toasters, blenders, and several answering machines. For whatever reason – I still don't know why – I decided to plug in the last answering machine my grandmother would have used. The micro-cassette played out loud. It was the sound of my brother Charles, singing with gusto from the classic Broadway musical *Oklahoma!* 'Oh, what a beautiful morning! Oh, what a beautiful day! I've got a wonderful feeling everything's going my way'. His laughter pealed out! He was convulsed with joy. And then he said, 'Hi! I just thought I'd call to say, "Hope you're having a good day!" I love you! Bye!' Here, in this space and time, Charles was alive. His voice was as real to me then as ever I'd known him. I was listening – in real time – to my brother. At that moment, I was given the gift of wonder. What higher power led me to turn on that one answering machine among a pile of random belongings?

Erik Aadahl, the Academy Award-nominated sound designer for *Argo* and *Transformers*, among other films, said, 'If you take a picture, it's just one moment frozen in time. But if you were to freeze sound, it would just be hash. You need to be rolling on, to actually hear a sound. In a sense, sound is more of a fourth dimension. It's very much tuned in to [how we] experience reality. I find that to be really profound.'

Gary Rydstrom is often asked to speak before groups of all kinds, and at the end of his presentation, he frequently poses this question: 'If you had to choose between a photograph or an aural recording of a loved one who has passed on, which would you choose?'

I asked each documentary interviewee that very same question. As each person reflected, either a tear came to their eye, or a delighted personal smile to their lips. I had the privilege of being able to pose the question to Robert Redford, who immediately said, quite matter-of-factly, 'Oh, the recording. A photograph can capture a look or mood from a moment. But the voice is unique. Each person's personal possession.' When I asked him, would he care to mention whom he wished he had an audio recording of, he shook his head. 'No,' he said, 'there are too many.' And he smiled.

Exercise: Create your own sound memories

Take the time to consider what major film storytellers have discovered about the power of sound to tap into our primal emotions and memories. Consider doing the following:

1. Try and remember a favourite sound memory from your childhood

Using an audio recording device, such as your smartphone, record a voice memo and tell yourself the story of what that sound means to you now. Or, if you can record that sound – for example, birdsong, a train signal, a commercial jingle, or church bell chime – record it now. These sounds may well pass away. Upon hearing them later, you will be cast back immediately to that time and place, and it will feel 'alive now'.

2. Create an aural recording of a loved one

Think about your nearest and dearest – relatives, friends, even a mentor. Again, using your smartphone, or any recording device, take a few minutes to capture their laughter or speaking voice.

Also consider recording the everyday chatter you hear around you. Record your children or nieces and nephews as they grow up. Just have them say a few things – you'll be very grateful to rehear their two-year-old or twelve-year-old voices and laughter much later on. Have your elders tell an anecdote or read a favourite poem aloud. Or simply capture your family chatting, laughing, eating a meal. I have a microcassette answering machine recording of my two-year-old cousin calling to ask me, in his garbled, toddler language, when was I coming to visit? But my favourite is my 85-year-old Great-Aunt Margie (who was born in 1898), who, upon realising that she was speaking into an answering machine, says sternly, 'You know, I don't like these machines ...' You cannot replicate these moments.

Once you have your recordings, simply label and upload these sound memories to your computer or the cloud, and maybe even add a photograph of the speaker.

3. Watch a classic film and focus on the sound design

Francis Ford Coppola said that 'sound is 50 per cent of the experience' of watching a movie. The next time you want to watch a film, choose one of the iconic sound-design breakthrough films I've listed in the Resources section at the end of the book. This time, as you view the film, listen for how the sound design – not just the music – and the silence are orchestrated to make your cinematic experience far more immersive and emotionally moving.

An idea,
like a ghost ...
must be spoken to
a little before it
will explain itself

—

Charles Dickens

3
When We Close Our Ears

What is it about the act of active listening that leads people to either a state of awe, astonishment or total resentment: 'Argh, that so-and-so made me listen for *hours* as they droned on!'

I grew up in a home where children were expected to be seen and not heard. My mother said I was a highly verbal baby and that she can't remember when I didn't talk. But around my father, I was expected to listen. He was a storyteller, a great entertainer, even an orator or polemicist who might have done exceptionally well had he entered the public arena as a politician or news commentator. Yet he became a public high school history teacher. Every night, at home, fuelled by Manhattan cocktails, he pontificated aloud, preparing his next-day lectures ... and at length, brooking no interference. I learned to listen well.

Of course, I took this nightly routine for granted. For years I thought everyone listened to their father for hours on end; I only realised later on that this was not common. Most times, my father was brilliant, being well-read in current events and was hilarious in his comic timing. Other times he was, well, overbearing.

Because I was seldom allowed to speak or be heard in his presence, I spoke plenty elsewhere. It wasn't until my 84-year-old father knew he was dying that the table for listening finally turned towards me. He asked for me to fly to see him immediately, and when I arrived by his side, he said that I could ask him anything I wanted to. I said, 'Why didn't you ever ask me about my life? Why didn't you ever let me speak?' He sighed. There was a long silence. Finally, he said, 'Because I envied you. You have the life I wished I had.' My conservative father had always revelled in the fact that he'd had a monthly income since the age of twenty. He was proud of his impeccable credit record. But at what cost, I thought? So, I told him about the financial risks I'd had to take in my freelance career. How I'd had to learn how to live way out on a limb, and develop nerves of steel to endure the negotiations I'd had with major players, learning to face them eyeball to eyeball. Nothing had prepared me for that. It was trial and error. But it was an inevitable course of action if I wanted my freelance career to advance. My father stared into the long distance, then very quietly, he said, 'You know, I could never have done that.' He paused. 'Thank you for telling me this.' That was our last conversation. He died the following day. The silence is deafening.

Listening is a gift – one we give to ourselves and also to others. When you listen, you always get far more back than you had going into the conversation. Simply put, you know more. I know full well what it's like to live in the oxygen-deprived presence of someone who loves the sound of their own voice, and I bet many of us are familiar with the feeling of being obligated to listen to someone due to their power over us – be that a family member, a boss, or any superior. You become numb by repeated exposure.

But listening does not have to be boring. Think of it as choosing to be in tune with others. It has been said that the problem with our current social media landscape is that we are each living in our own silos, each of us in our own self-selected 'filter bubbles'. We only want to listen to those who are like us.

But if we choose to not listen to what makes us uncomfortable, how will we ever grow? How can a democracy exist without debate, negotiation and compromise? Our current democratic process might appear to be broken beyond repair, but there is still much of value in its ideals.

When we're not listening, we're not communicating. And a lack of communication often leads to anger and mistrust. In a 2017 *Esquire*/NBC national survey poll of three thousand American adults, it was found that half were angrier than they were the previous year. And if you were in the US in 2016, people were very angry then as the presidential election revealed the gaping chasms of our fractured democracy. Political analysts and pollsters said they'd never seen anything like it. As a microcosm of the social atmosphere, I remember seeing an episode of CBS's *60 Minutes* on which a diverse group of Americans was gathered together to discuss various political issues. The protocol was that each person would take a turn responding to questions posed by the moderator, but what ended up happening was that everyone started shouting all at once. Ranting. On camera. All at the same time, with no one – not one person – giving any quarter. The commentator said there seemed to be no way to get them to stop and listen to each other before speaking.

Around this time, David Wolpe, Senior Rabbi of the Sinai Temple in Los Angeles, said in *TIME* magazine:

Angry people are poor communicators and even worse listeners. Their empathy is foreshortened, and they have trouble imagining the other's point of view. It makes people less healthy, and when both parties are angry, fewer are likely to find middle ground. If the only way people feel they will be heard is when they are angry, then our public discourse will be an arena for shouting past one another. Now that a sanctified modern method, a poll, has shown we're angry, perhaps we can have a reasoned public discussion about how to calm the rage and begin the work. You can be principled even when you speak in a soft voice.

First came the shock of the UK Brexit Referendum on 23 June 2016, when 52 per cent voted to leave the European Union; then came the results of the US Presidential election in November 2016.

Within eight months of the first year of the 45th president's four-year term, Americans witnessed white supremacists march in a tiki-torch parade while shouting Nazi slogans like 'Blood and soil' on the lawn of Thomas Jefferson's beloved University of Virginia. They were protesting the removal of the statue of Confederate General Robert E. Lee. In their Unite the Right rally on 12 August 2017, tensions escalated with the arrival of counter-protestors, and more than a dozen people were injured in physical altercations. An angry white male supremacist sympathiser drove his car into the crowd, killing one of the protestors, 32-year-old Heather Heyer, and injuring many others.

All of us have been forced to figure out how we got to this place. One defining factor has been the rise of social media – in particular Facebook and Twitter – whose potential dangers have been amplified by the suspicion, and very real possibility, that foreign nations may have used these channels to meddle in the democratic elections of both the United States and the United Kingdom.

As Annie Proulx, author of *Brokeback Mountain*, said in her National Book Award speech on 16 November 2017:

> This is a Kafkaesque time ... We observe social media's manipulation of a credulous population, a population dividing into bitter tribal cultures. We are living through a massive shift from representative democracy to something called viral direct democracy, now cascading over us in a garbage-laden tsunami of raw data. Everything is situational, seesawing between gut-response 'like' or vicious confrontations. For some this is a heady time of brilliant technological innovation that is bringing us into an exciting new world. For others it is the opening of a savagely difficult book without a happy ending.

Where is the soft voice? Where is the listening? How do we find a happy ending?

Exercise: The practice of 'mindful listening'

Can you think of a time when someone said to you, 'You're not listening to me!' How do you view that encounter now? Were you preoccupied, anxious or angry at the time? Can you find compassion for yourself and that event now?

The next time you get into a simple argument or misunderstanding with your partner, spouse, friend, or a work colleague, just stop the discussion for a moment and do the following:

— Restate the ideas and feelings of the person who is upset. Try to do so accurately, until they are satisfied. Ask that person to do the same for you.

Sounds simple, doesn't it? Yet this will be difficult, in part because you will be stating the other person's point of view before your own. But if you practise this mindful listening process with those closest to you, it will become a known pattern. You will be creating an environment of trust. Everyone will feel heard. You will become known as someone who listens well, as opposed to a know-it-all.

New things usually happen after you do this.

Out beyond ideas
of wrongdoing
and rightdoing
there is a field.
I'll meet you there.
When the soul
lies down in that grass,
the world is too full
to talk about

—

Rumi

It takes a great man
to be a good listener

—

Calvin Coolidge

4
And So It Begins

You never really understand a person until you consider things from his point of view ... until you climb into his skin and walk around in it.

—

Atticus Finch, *To Kill a Mockingbird*

Sometimes, when things seem utterly hopeless, we hear an unlikely story. In December 2017, this came from CNN reporters Mallory Simon and Sara Sidner.

At a courthouse in Charlottesville, Virginia, Billy Snuffer – the Imperial Wizard of the Rebel Brigade Knights (aka the Ku Klux Klan) – was there with other Klansmen. They were attending the trial of one of their colleagues charged with shooting a gun during the Unite the Right rally, the same protest where Heather Heyer was killed by the charging car.

Angry protestors shouted down the Klansmen as they attempted to enter the courthouse. Into this melee walked 59-year-old Daryl Davis, a blues musician and descendant of African slaves. As protestors screamed vitriol from the sidelines – one African-American woman said, 'You're a person of colour; why the hell are you talking to them?' to which Davis replied, 'That's right, I am a person of colour, but I'm an American and so is this man right here' – Davis shook Snuffer's hand, saying, 'What's going on, man, how're you doing?' The men embraced.

Daryl Davis has made it his life's work to befriend Klansmen. Many times, he is the first black person they have actually spoken to. This journey began for him when he was a ten-year-old boy, facing racism in Belmont, a suburb of Boston. Even then he wondered, 'How can they hate me? They don't even know me.'

He began to seek out Klan members. He has been attacked and kicked. His modus operandi? He says that mostly he just listens – even as they spew hatred. He listens, thinks, and then responds, and he has been doing so for more than thirty years.

Over time, he has inspired many of these Klansmen to leave the group, and when they do, they give him their robes. At Davis's home, there are dozens of KKK robes and memorabilia, hanging on his walls like museum artefacts. Not because he demanded or cajoled for them. He says they were given to him by people who had learned from him. All he did, he says modestly, was to try to reach a middle ground. He looks around at all the robes, arranging the opulent cowls and belts, and, of course, the hoods, saying, 'They're done. They're done. As a result of meeting me and having these conversations. Not overnight, but over time.'

Walking alongside Billy Snuffer at the Charlottesville courthouse, Davis knew all too well that they made an unlikely couple. This was their second meeting. Davis was trying to find some common ground. They discussed the Klan, Nazis and hate. Even before the CNN camera came to capture their story, Davis got Snuffer to admit that the Unite the Right rally was not about the removal of a Confederate general's statue. Davis said, 'This was all about starting a race war.' Snuffer agreed, 'You're exactly right.' As Davis listened, he was ever mindful of the KKK's history of lynching, raping and terrorising.

Members of the NAACP (National Association for the Advancement of Coloured People) have derided Davis for associating with any member of the KKK. But Davis sees this as his life mission. Davis believes that to make change happen, 'you have to find some brotherhood.' At the courthouse that day, Davis appealed to the judge to consider sending the Klansman on trial to the National Museum of African American History and Culture in Washington, DC, in the way that courts mandate education for first-time offenders. Davis sat in the courtroom alongside Snuffer for two hours. His hope was that Snuffer would remember that Davis was decent that day. The Imperial Wizard witnessed a black man stand up for him against angry protestors.

When Davis got home that night, his phone rang. Billy Snuffer asked him if he made it home all right. As Davis organised his room full of hanging robes given to him by Klansmen he had befriended, he reflected on his conversations with Snuffer, and the potential there was that, in listening, he might change someone's heart and mind: 'And so it begins.'

The story of such a man as Daryl Davis heartens me. By all accounts, he is an ordinary citizen. For more than thirty years, he has taken his own free time to seek out his enemy and simply try to reach out to him, by listening. What an extraordinary thing to do. And, yet, what else can we do in a democracy but agree to disagree? To try and find a way to 'get on, by getting along'. Surely, this is how democracies have risen to such heights of progress for the common good.

I take heart in what historian and activist Howard Zinn said in his book *A People's History of the United States*. And I quote:

> What matters are the countless small deeds of unknown people who lay the basis of the significant events that enter history. They're the ones who have done it in the past. They're the ones who will have to do it in the future.

Listening takes time. You must pause, take a moment, and offer yourself to another person, with your full attention. Honestly, sometimes this can feel like a drag. Maybe their issue will inconvenience you. Maybe they're confused or in emotional pain. But there will be times when listening will be the most important thing you will ever do.

Exercise: A 5-minute listening practice

Someone once said that we should never underestimate the 5-minute conversation with a 16-year-old. Can you find five minutes to give to someone – perhaps someone you know you *should* listen to more, or someone who simply needs your time and focus, even just for a few minutes? Simply listen to the other person without judging, or reacting with your eyes or sighs or any audible reactions.

See what happens ...

Kindness is a language
that the deaf can hear
and the blind can see

Mark Twain

When people talk, listen completely

—

Ernest Hemingway

5
To Listen is an Active Verb

The word 'listen' contains the same letters as the word 'silent'.

Alfred Brendel, KBE

When you open your awareness to others, and the world, a new kind of radar seems to plug in. You develop 'ears to hear' in a way that is more alive. Whether that's the vast array of birds calling in the great animal orchestra, no matter where you live, or the frantic sounds of sirens coming from just around the corner, or the tone of your loved one's voice – their sorrow or delight – in developing ears to hear, you become more aware.

It's like a kind of fine-tuning – a strengthening of your senses – no less than exercising to keep up your physical health, or learning a language or complex art, craft or skill to keep your brain in tip-top shape. Once you learn to tune in, you are changed forever. And you are much the better for it. Listening is an everyday act, at once ordinary and majestic. It is also an act of great generosity.

So powerful is this act that consciously choosing *not* to listen can generate great harm. It can harm not only yourself as you tune out and cut yourself off from others – sleepwalking through life and gradually losing touch with your own humanity – but potentially harm other people, too.

Such is the tragic, true story of the murder of 28-year-old Kitty Genovese, who was walking home from her night job in the early hours of 13 March 1964. She was just at her apartment door in Queens, a borough of New York City, when she was approached from behind. She was stabbed repeatedly, even as she screamed loudly for help, shouting, 'Oh my God he stabbed me! Help me!'

It was reported that many of her neighbours heard her cries for help. They closed their blinds. Someone did shout out the window, 'Let that girl alone!' but to no avail. After the attacker, later identified as Winston Moseley, stabbed her, he stole $49 from her wallet and left her on the doorstep. Kitty stumbled into the lobby but was so seriously injured, she couldn't open her locked apartment door. Still, she continued to cry for help, whereupon Moseley returned. This time, now inside the building, he stabbed her again, and then raped her, before fleeing the scene. During all this, two people apparently did call the police. Then, a neighbour, Sophia Farrar, ventured out and cradled Kitty until the ambulance arrived. Kitty died on the way to the hospital. One person famously said later, 'I didn't want to get involved.'

In the aftermath of the crime, Kitty's neighbours and the press seemed indifferent to the event until the New York City Police Commissioner, Michael J. Murphy, sought out Abe Rosenthal, the metropolitan editor of the *New York Times*, saying, 'The Queens story is one for the books.' Soon after, the newspaper published an investigative report written by Martin Gansberg, with the headline, '37 Who Saw Murder and Didn't Call the Police'.

This event has become a standard example in social studies and psychology textbooks. The response – or non-response – of Kitty Genovese's neighbours is now termed the 'Bystander Effect' or 'Genovese Syndrome'. Over time, the story entered popular culture as a portrait of urban indifference, and it has been mythologised in television programmes, books and songs. In recent years, more analysis has revealed that the original *New York Times* report was flawed; in particular the number of 'witnesses' was found to be a gross exaggeration. And yet the bystander effect is still a force in human interaction. As professor Harold Takooshian wrote in 2004 in *Psychology Today*, 'When the Chief of Detectives Albert Seedman asked him [Winston Moseley] how he dared to attack a woman in front of so many witnesses, the psychopath calmly replied, "I knew they wouldn't do anything, people never do."' Moseley confessed to not only Kitty's murder but two other fatal attacks nearby.

The witnesses' lack of response is attributed to what psychologists call *diffusion of responsibility*, a socio-psychological phenomenon when people in groups of three or more are less likely to act responsibly. This phenomenon has also been used to explain the behaviour of European citizens who failed to act during the countless World War Two atrocities carried out by the Nazis.

When you listen to a witness, you become a witness.

Elie Wiesel

Listening can become a responsibility – a call to action to save another person's life, a revelation of humanity. And that's when listening reveals character. Throughout history, we have stories of individuals who listened and responded to the call to action, no matter their own personal pain and loss, and we remember and honour them to this day.

Learning to listen means you're becoming mature, a true adult. You may well discover your life's purpose. You will experience what it is to become fully alive. But over time, this one thing has proven to be equally true: Denying what you hear – cutting off the call to action – will inexorably lead to a person becoming lost to themselves forever.

My mandate going into the Weinstein story was never to *believe* all survivors; it was to *listen* to all survivors. I think it's completely possible to be both a sceptical, judicious reporter and also create a space for survivors to be heard. If that reporting inspires people to activism, then it's a job done well.

Ronan Farrow, *The Hollywood Reporter*, 10 Jan. 2018

On 5 October 2017, the *New York Times* published an investigative report by Jodi Kantor and Megan Twohey about Hollywood mogul Harvey Weinstein's sexual harassment pattern – his widely known abuse of power, and the complicity machine that surrounded him. A few days later, the first of reporter Ronan Farrow's in-depth articles gave his well-known victims more time to speak. These stories rocked Hollywood and led to an industry-wide reckoning. Within just three months, the silence was shattered in a way it hadn't been before, with the #MeToo movement, which inspired women to come forward and expose via social media the powerful men who had sexually harassed them. Farrow's article in the *New Yorker* (6 November 2017) led to the unparalleled downfall of Harvey Weinstein. He was charged and convicted of rape and sexual assault in March 2020, and was sentenced to 23 years in prison. More #MeToo stories from high-profile women continued to spill out about other industry titans.

A cascade of public firings has ensued. Women are marching. We are now witnessing a major cultural shift, led by the idea of listening.

Most of the men outed by their accusers denied any wrongdoing. Some said they had been misrepresented; that it was a case of consensual sex, and now they were experiencing 'political hit jobs' (a term coined by former Fox News star Bill O'Reilly). Some acknowledged the pain they caused, but without really apologising to their victims.

But Louis CK, a prominent comedian, came out immediately with a fresh new take. He responded to his six accusers, saying, 'These stories are true.' People were surprised by his frankness. He acknowledged his abuse of power and how perverse and one-sided his perspective was. Then, he concluded his statement with, 'I have spent my long and lucky career talking and saying anything I want. I will now step back and take a long time to listen.' The last word, finally. *Listen.*

The #MeToo movement has swept the entertainment and media industry, taking down even its lasting icons.

Charlie Rose was an anchor of *CBS This Morning* and the host and producer of the PBS show *Charlie Rose* since 1991. The 76-year-old could talk to anyone and was considered the embodiment of the gracious conversationalist who made everyone – especially the audience – feel welcome at his round oak table. Using the same MeToo hashtag, a number of women reported a pattern of sexual advances by Rose when they were young interns or employees invited to his elegant estate and CBS News immediately fired Rose, and PBS cancelled his show.

The takedown of such a high-profile and widely respected personality would have been unheard of even just a year ago. Social media had a newfound purpose and cause. With #MeToo, women would no longer be silenced.

The day after Rose's firing, his CBS morning-news co-host, Gayle King, was asked to appear on the station's *Late Show with Steven Colbert*. There was a very sensitive moment between them on camera.

Colbert has been a long-standing comedic foil and he easily stepped into the role of highlighting the follies and foibles of the many powerful men who abused their position by harassing women. He was equally merciless to Charlie Rose, especially when it came to Rose's age and the very young women he continually seemed to hire to work on his PBS show. Gayle King was not pleased at the laughter Colbert gleaned at Rose's expense. Colbert said, 'What is it that you think we men should now do?' She said she was angry and numb and seemed genuinely flummoxed. She didn't know how to answer. But then she acknowledged, 'Well, even though Charlie Rose was my friend, and I have always admired him, I cannot stop thinking about those young women. He does not get a pass on this one. It's time women are believed. We really need to know that men come into the conversation or nothing can change.'

Colbert: 'Well, what's the best way for men to join the conversation other than listen and believe?'

King agreed: 'To listen and say it's not going to be tolerated.'

Suddenly, listening had become a very important part of the conversation when it came to power politics. The implication is that when you listen your heart becomes open to change. You see the world from a perspective other than your own.

When I was growing up, it seemed as if every classic Western featured the line, 'You can never truly understand a man, until you've walked a mile in his moccasins'. The point is to understand a person before judging them. This very sentiment became a theme of the civil rights movement in the 1960s, and it is equally relevant to the worldwide #MeToo movement.

On 9 February 2018, *Quartz*, a sister publication of *The Atlantic*, published the first in a four-part series on gender equality. 'The Visionaries' featured interviews with '50 of the world's most qualified and ambitious women across every industry about how they achieved their success … from Sheryl Sandberg and Tarana Burke to Emily Weiss and Zhang Xin'. When the women in the series were asked what they wanted from men, the resounding answer was, 'Just listen to us.'

Indeed, this 'advent of listening' presaged a new era of civility, and an inherent willingness to believe in a woman's side of the story.

It takes two
to speak the truth:
one to speak
and one to listen

—

Henry David Thoreau

6
Listening Brings Truth

'Listen to your life as it whispers to you.' Oprah Winfrey
often speaks of this, her abiding life principle. She says,
'In all my years of doing *The Oprah Show*, I wanted to say
it a thousand times. My staff counted, and told me I'd
said it only 33 times. But I was thinking it all the time.'
How often do we listen to ourselves? That still small
voice that, perhaps, speaks the truth. And if we did,
what might we learn? Where might it lead us?

We know Oprah as a self-made billionaire and leading
cultural force, but to fully understand her success, it
is worth looking at her formative early years. She talks
freely about her young life: how she was raised by her
grandmother in poor, rural Mississippi; the shame she
endured as an unwed pregnant teenager whose baby died
shortly after birth; her longing to be an actress; and her
strivings to fit in as a television reporter – in spite of her
TV news boss saying she was 'too too' – meaning, she
put 'too much' of herself into the story, on camera, as a
professional reporter. To fill out the last months of her
contract, he eventually gave her an afternoon talk show in
Baltimore, and soon after she had a major breakthrough.
She desperately wanted to act in the 1985 film *The Color*

Purple, believing that Alice Walker's novel was really *her* story. When a casting director came to Chicago, Oprah was able to audition for the role of Sofia. But after the audition, she heard nothing. Finally, she called the casting director's office in Hollywood. He told her in no uncertain terms that she had no business calling him. He said he was in the process of auditioning a very experienced, well-known actress for the role, because, as she well knew, Steven Spielberg would be directing the film. Crestfallen, Oprah went away to a weight-loss camp, or 'fat farm' as she called it.

While out jogging, she listened to *that* whisper, deep inside her, and knew that she had to let go of her deep desires if she wanted to be happy. She would bless the actress who would get the job. It was all she could do to 'let go'. As she tells the story, she said she began to sing the gospel song, 'I Surrender All'. And then suddenly she heard a voice shouting from outside the weight-loss facility. There was an important call for her in the main office. Oprah raced inside to find Steven Spielberg on the phone. He offered her the role, adding that he didn't want her to lose any weight. Overjoyed, Oprah drove home that day and stopped by Dairy Queen to enjoy her favourite ice-cream treat to celebrate. How could an overweight African-American woman dare to believe she could be a movie star? To this day, she says, she starts each day by listening, meditating, taking time apart.

In her recent book, *Beyond the Label: Women, Leadership, and Success on Our Own Terms*, Maureen Chiquet, former global CEO of Chanel, speaks about the unlikely trajectory of her successful rise in retail from Gap to Old Navy to Chanel – or, as she puts it, from 'mass to class' – because she learned how to listen.

Mickey Drexler, then CEO of Gap was Chiquet's dynamic boss. She says that 'Mickey Meetings' were the stuff of lore, their purpose being to attain his approval and sign-off on the final product assortments and buying plans for the next season. There was a reason that Wall Street called Drexler the 'merchant prince': he had a near-perfect batting average at picking bestsellers. In one meeting in particular, Chiquet wanted to show that she was not afraid to take risks and was eager to reveal her 'new secret weapon – a fantastic new fabric in a trendy new fit'. But during the meeting Drexler's passionate, volatile ripostes only made her defend her choices harder. Finally, he told her that he couldn't stand there and argue with her anymore – she wasn't listening. With that, he stormed out of the meeting. When she got back to her office, Drexler called her. She braced herself. Was she about to be fired? Instead, he told her she had potential, good taste, and an eye for bestsellers. But, he told her, she had to learn to listen. 'I am just asking you to stop, open your ears and hear what people have to say. If you don't, you'll never be a great merchant ... You need to listen better.'

When he hung up, Chiquet realised what a big lesson she had just been given by the CEO of one of the most successful retail companies in America. Chiquet writes: 'He cared enough to teach me one of the most important lessons I would ever learn. To listen. To listen deeply.' In that moment, Chiquet realised that if she wanted to succeed in business and in life she would have to practise listening.

Chiquet went on to become one of the top merchants at Gap and was then given the opportunity to build Old Navy as a great new brand in mass consumer retail. As her star rose, management asked her to complete an assessment to review any gaps in her leadership. She would be soliciting feedback from the people around her: direct reports, peers, and bosses. The assessment came back overall very favourable. One detail that emerged, however, was that her colleagues loved to learn from her but also suggested that she ask them their opinions and take time to consider where they were coming from. The woman who was sharing the results of the assessment with Maureen told her, 'I want you to appreciate what you do well but this is about seeing yourself from another's perspective.'

What tough medicine, but great wisdom: to dare to see ourselves as others see us. Most of us wouldn't want to know. But as the late great Scottish poet Robert Burns wrote, 'O wad some Power the giftie gie us To see oursels as ithers see us', or, in modern English, 'O, for the power who can give us the gift to see ourselves as others see us!'

Chiquet took this assessment to heart. She changed her approach. Soon, armed with her new leadership skills, she was named president of Banana Republic. Around this time Chiquet was also being courted by major headhunters; all she knew about it was that a top luxury brand was looking for a new global CEO. She took various meetings over a couple of years but thought no more about it until she was offered the opportunity to become the global CEO for Chanel, Inc. The transition came with this caveat: she had to spend three full years of training before taking on complete responsibility. In particular, she was asked to do nothing but listen. For an entire year. This would allow her to garner intelligence from the company's highly seasoned and tenured employees and develop an appreciation of and respect for the creative process.

'My willingness to let go of my need to prove myself and embrace this silent period as an opportunity to learn (albeit frustrating at times) helped me earn the trust of my new team members whose experience and expertise were much deeper than mine ... It required patience and humility,' said Chiquet. She could see that taking leadership would not be about espousing a grand vision or waving a flag, but that she had to ask a lot of questions. And as she listened to their answers, she would 'listen for what tensions and concern lay just under the surface.' It was a type of curiosity that became contagious. Her team began to ask more focused questions. Finally, she realised that, as a company, they would have to listen much more to their customers, their employees and the world around them.

When Chiquet was free to lead Chanel into a whole new era – combining her expertise in online retail, social media and appealing to a new generation of mass consumers with the mystique of Chanel's couture-class appeal – she had an Aha! moment. She had gone too far in the wrong direction. 'I was listening too much to everyone else and, as a consequence, I [was] left feeling unanchored from the vision and values I knew we needed to forge ahead. My team could see it, too ... I'd been so focused on empathising with others that I risked losing my way as their leader.' This would seem to be an all-too-common complaint of women leaders, and Chiquet knew it.

She then found her way to a rather unorthodox coach: horse whisperer, Koelle Simpson, based in California. In the theory of horse-human relationships, it is said that the horse mirrors the human. They take their cue from us, and reflect back who we are. They either follow you or they don't. (See the documentary film, *Buck*, directed by Cindy Meehl, for the true story of the man who inspired Robert Redford's *The Horse Whisperer*.) Through her work with Simpson, Chiquet was able to look at herself through a new lens; she came home to the truth of who she really was. And she believed in herself as a leader.

Chiquet returned to Chanel, now more confident and fully integrated in both sides of the values of listening.

She was able to say, 'Real authority comes when you are able to strike the right balance. You need to listen to others, and you need to be attuned to yourself.'

She went on to lead Chanel through major market disruptions, upheavals and creative innovations. Today, the company thrives as the top luxury brand for the 21st century across all retail platforms – a feat very few luxury brands have been able to achieve, let alone expand upon or even maintain. In 2016, Chiquet decided to leave Chanel, proud of what she had accomplished, not sure what her next adventure will be. But one thing she knew was that she had to listen to her inner voice and be true to herself.

Deep Listening

Both Oprah and Maureen have attained that all-too-rare pinnacle for women today: they became leaders whose influence transformed their chosen fields. They achieved this by applying the principles of 'deep listening'.

As Oprah said in her Harvard University commencement address in 2013: 'I have to say that the single most important lesson I learned in 25 years talking to people every single day, was that there is one common denominator. We want to be validated. We want to be understood. After 35,000 interviews, as soon as the camera shut off, everyone turned to me and inevitably asked, "Was that okay?" I heard that from President Bush, President Obama, even Beyoncé. Friends and family, your enemies, strangers in every encounter, in every exchange, they want to know this one thing: Was that okay? Did you hear me? Did what I say mean anything to you?'

As she ended her historic Harvard address she said, 'But I know this one thing for sure, if you're willing to listen to, be guided by, that still small voice that is the GPS within yourself, to find out what makes you come alive, you will be more than okay. You will be happy, you will be successful, and you will make a difference in the world.'

She concluded: 'Congratulations, Class of 2013. Thank you for listening. Was that okay?'

A key part of deep listening is the courage and the willingness to see ourselves as others see us – which can be both mortifying and deeply gratifying – and then to still listen to the truth of who we really are. Listening always leads us to this wisdom: Be true to who you really are.

Exercise: Deep listening in 5 minutes

What if you set aside five minutes – alone – to just listen to yourself?

Make this *your* time. Switch off or set aside any distractions – phone, computer, TV, and so on. You may say you're too busy, but perhaps you can incorporate this exercise into something you're already doing. For example, see if you can give yourself five extra minutes to sit in the car before you head in to work or pick up your children.

Ideally you want to find a safe, quiet space. If not the car, this could be a favourite armchair, a park bench, or – again – go on a short walk. Try and take yourself away from the normal hustle and bustle.

Look up and around. Find *one beautiful thing* to focus on – the sky, clouds, a tree – then:

— Pause. Just listen. You will hear a rattling of thoughts, lists, worries – this is what meditation gurus call your 'monkey mind'.

— Allow your monkey mind to flow past you for a minute or two. Acknowledge any 'white noise', the irritating sound of a lawnmower or faraway noise you can't control. Ignore it all.

— Only. Listen. To. Yourself.

— Breathe in seven beats. Breathe out eleven beats. Repeat for one minute.

— Focus on your breath. If your mind drifts, choose just one word to guide you back to your breath – make it a positive word. If you are afraid, anxious or angry, feel free to shout, scream (yes, that's allowed!) Just let it all out.

— Then breathe. And Listen.

This will be difficult at first. You will become easily distracted or bored. But if you can give yourself five minutes a day for 180 days, this practice *will* change your life. Like strengthening a muscle, see if you can work up to twenty minutes, interspersed throughout the day. Create a pattern. This is an intention – a promise to yourself.

After time and practice, you can expect your 'monkey mind' to filter down. All the irritating thoughts will settle like silt in a rushing river until the water clears and you can see everything. You will have clarity. And you will – at last – hear the 'still, small voice' of your deep inner wisdom that's been whispering to you all along.

Listening happens in time. Take the time to set yourself apart from the noise and distractions, and welcome what you might be able to hear in the silence.

And what
happened next?

7
How We Learn to Listen Differently

If a man does not keep pace with his companions, perhaps it is because he hears a different drummer. Let him step to the music which he hears, however measured or far away.

Henry David Thoreau

Listening is the foundation for respect, for the right of the other person to be different. In my case, it wasn't a person who taught me this lesson. It was my dog. Luna is a very beautiful, smart tri-colour Shetland sheepdog, also known as a Sheltie. When she took over my life as a four-month-old puppy, I was completely unprepared and overwhelmed. My parents had never allowed us to have pets. They had grown up on farms full of animals – cows, pigs, horses and, yes, cats and dogs – yet their philosophy was that animals should never be domesticated; they belonged on farms where they could roam free. Nevertheless, my three brothers and I each got ourselves a dog and a cat when we left home.

But I was completely flummoxed by the demands of this little puppy. Why couldn't she behave like my cat? Be independent, take care of her own business, walk thin, sit fat. Instead Luna spoke to me – at length – in a wild and foreign language of yelps, pips, growls and barks. A herding animal, she was always attempting to get me to do something I didn't understand. I didn't know how to respond. (Okay, I sound like a terrible owner. I know, I know ...) I kept thinking that I needed to behave like the alpha in the pack; then she would follow my lead. But no, there was some other communication bandwidth we would have to find together, if we were ever to have a happy home. For one, I hadn't realised what a responsibility it was to have to walk her three, even four times a day! Cats didn't need this kind of attention ... Plus, Luna didn't really walk. Rather, she dawdled, taking her sweet time to smell every single new daily *drop of information* left by her fellow dogs. This also meant that I had to speak to strangers, or rather fellow dog lovers, whose dogs always wanted to play with Luna. On a regular basis I was impatient, bored even, until I began to notice that the other dog lovers were amused by Luna's cute, playful romping.

Then one day, while we were out on the street, she stopped, sat bolt upright, and then began to howl. Across the crowded street – literally full of dogs of every breed imaginable – Luna spied the only male Sheltie in the neighbourhood, the very handsome Robbie, I was soon to learn. Robbie raced across the street, his owner, M'Leigh, in tow. For Robbie and Luna, it was kismet. They leapt high in the air, bumped their chests, and chewed each other's ears while circling round and round. In short, it was love at first sight. Thereafter, Luna pawed and chirped at me in a very special way every single day whenever she sensed that Robbie was nearby. And she was always right!

I began to learn the language of Luna. Dog-behaviour scientists say that shepherd dogs, as a breed, can learn up to one thousand words or commands in our language. But, equally so, I tuned in to her specific barks. I learned the difference between her whimper when she was thirsty and her whine to go outside, and her sneezes of delight when a favourite friend came to visit. As I opened up to her, she encouraged me to slow down and take the time to walk, look and listen. Before long a new world had opened up to me: the dawn chorus of Southern California, the whoosh of the ravens and the wild parrots cawing throughout the day, and, in the night, the raucous, howling coyotes. As I tuned into her worldview, I perceived her extra-sensory awareness of danger – far-off sirens or an approaching skateboarder – or of promise – as with the heady sound of a plastic bag being ever-so-quietly pulled open: a dog treat, for sure, beckoned. She would bound in, her fluffy white tail waving high at full mast. My world expanded when I accepted our differences. She became a very happy, well-adjusted dog. And I met my neighbours.

Listening can feel like walking into a vast park. It creates a wide open space to find common ground among strangers. There is no other way but by and through *listening* that we can find similarities. While you are crossing the barrier of your own ego by listening to another's point of view, you are also creating an opening in order to find a new way forward – a new hope in the world.

History continually reveals that revolutions – whether violent or peaceful – take place when someone speaks truth into the age in such a way that people can 'develop an imagination' to embrace a wholly new worldview.

One such person was Muhammad Ali. He ushered in a phenomenal era of American sportsmanship in the 1960s, that also coincided with the efforts towards racial equality as put forth in the civil rights movement. Muhammad Ali's birth name was Cassius Clay, after the highly revered albeit eccentric nineteenth-century abolitionist. The Clay who would become Muhammad Ali rose up out of total obscurity, hailing from a poor neighbourhood in Louisville, Kentucky, and then bursting onto the world scene at the age of sixteen with extraordinary bravado, self-confidence and boxing talent. The young Cassius Clay won an Olympic gold medal in Rome in 1960, and one year later, he became a professional heavyweight boxer. At age 22, he won the heavyweight championship of the world. He shouted over and over, 'I AM THE GREATEST!' Clay intuitively understood the power of PR, and he charmed the world with his quotable poetry, memorably explaining his pugilistic tactics with the line, 'I'm going to float like a butterfly, and sting like a bee.' A year later, Clay converted to Islam and changed his name to Muhammad Ali.

As his star rose, Ali believed he could change the world's view of his skin colour. He would come on a television show and then interrupt the interviewer by saying, 'Ain't I pretty? Tell everyone I'm pretty.' While everyone laughed, the interviewer would agree that, yes, Ali was quite good-looking. Ali's charm offensive was masterful: African-Americans had always been judged by their appearance – now Ali was asking to be praised for how he looked. He was as fast a wit in an interview as he was in the ring.

From the time of Ali's arrival on the scene in the 1960s, everyone was astounded by how masterfully he took to the world stage. *And they listened*. He was admired by the press – not just the sports broadcasters – and often quoted. They were bowled over by his self-possession, his power of presentation.

During his sports reign, the sheer audacity of how Muhammad Ali carried himself mesmerised a young boy from Long Island. Billy Crystal, a short, white Jewish guy, adored Ali, the tall commanding African-American from the South. Crystal studied Ali for hours to understand his voice, his inflections, and his cadence – he listened carefully to how Ali spoke his truth.

Crystal was especially taken with the great duo of Ali and legendary sports commentator Howard Cosell. The two powerhouses were famous for their verbal jousting in interviews, and Crystal deeply admired how they both reshaped America's view of diversity, class and race – just by being great showmen. Crystal began to perform a 'duet skit' impersonating Cosell and Ali in comedy clubs around New York City, and the act in turn uplifted Cosell's interviews with Muhammad Ali; as a kind of counter-punch, further setting up Ali's comedic persona. Crystal's act remains today a masterpiece of the high art of interpretation – going far beyond comedy or impersonation.

Then, one day in 1974, Billy was asked to be the keynote speaker at a major event honouring Ali. It was make-or-break time for Crystal, who was nervous as hell. His mimicry was entirely based on how well he had listened to – and internalised the truth of – who Ali was as a man. And Crystal understood Ali, with a mysterious kind of depth and appreciation for how Ali was transforming America. When Crystal came on, Ali couldn't believe what he was hearing. Crystal commanded the evening. He brought down the house, as they say, and he did it not just with sidesplitting laughter but with a standing ovation based on astonishment and awe. Ali called him over and said, 'You're my brother now. My little brother.' The men remained close until Ali's death in 2016.

When Ali died at the age of 74, the nation mourned. His funeral was broadcast live. Former President Bill Clinton spoke. President Barack Obama sent a video with his condolences. For more than three hours, world leaders in politics, charity, sports and the Muslim world extolled Ali's impact and achievements.

The last speaker was Ali's beloved wife, Lonnie Ali. But the second to last speaker was Billy Crystal. It would be Crystal's last great impersonation of Ali. We longed to hear Ali's distinctive voice one last time. Crystal peppered his moving eulogy with perfectly executed imitations of the late Ali. After years of careful listening, Crystal was in tune with who Muhammad Ali was as both a man and a legend; Crystal had perfected the dance of listening. His ability to precisely and truthfully convey Ali demonstrates the power of true listening: when we tune into others' stories and internalise their truths, we see them for who they really are and they teach us to see the world in a new way.

Exercise: Who do you listen to?

We are, all of us, always listening to someone who is influencing our life – for good or bad. Use the following exercise to better understand the figures that impact your life.

1. Reflect on who you have been listening to. Who has influenced you in ways you've never consciously acknowledged? Think about rock stars, sports stars, cultural leaders, poets, performers, politicians, preachers, activists. Maybe you've listened to some bad influencers, or people you've now outgrown; perhaps you can now perceive their influence with new eyes and ears.

2. Who has made you see the world differently and influenced or even changed you? Do you still listen to that person? Do you hand off their thoughts or worldview to others you encounter? Is this what you *want* to do?

3. Who would you listen to now if you could? Revisit some classic recordings: the speeches of Martin Luther King, Jr, Gandhi and Winston Churchill; interviews with Mother Teresa; Marian Anderson singing at the foot of the Abraham Lincoln Memorial; J.K. Rowling reading *Harry Potter* ... there are so many. See the Resources section at the back of the book for details on where to find some.

   Take your time. Listen to how, from the timbre of their voice, they're teaching you something new even today. When we hear recordings from the past, they become alive again, strike us anew, and provide our hearts and minds with fresh insight.

Listening is
the foundation
of respect

8
The Foundation of Respect

A viral Facebook thread I saw recently posed the question: 'Is it possible that an idea is valid if you don't agree with it?' The post went on to ask, 'Can you think of a time recently when – even if you didn't agree with the other person – you realised that their position was just as valid as yours, you just didn't agree with it?'

There ensued a very long thread in which some said that it was impossible to accept an idea as valid if you didn't agree with it, while others equivocated, saying that maybe it was possible, but it hadn't happened to them. A few said that Facebook was no forum for real discourse. And, as is now all too common, a few snarky remarks were left too. Still, the question generated a lot of discussion from all angles.

When I think about the clash between strongly opposed viewpoints, I'm reminded of the TV show *All in the Family*, created by one of the great American television producers, Norman Lear. The series ran from 1971 to 1979, at a time when the country was perhaps far more polarised than it is even today. Lear created the series during the Vietnam War culture crisis, and the cast of characters featured the now infamous outspoken blue-collar arch-conservative Archie Bunker, played by Carroll O'Connor, who was set up in opposition to his shaggy-haired, denim-wearing liberal son-in-law, Meathead, played by Rob Reiner. In every episode, Archie gets ramped up into a terrible row with his son-in-law and/or his long-suffering wife, Edith, until he shouts, 'Stifle yourself!' Of course, we, the audience were able to see the real story as we watched this unashamed racist, sexist man struggle with the way the world was changing. In perhaps the most iconic episode, Meathead finds himself, yet again, trying to shout some sense into Archie. But Archie blocks his every comment, by singing 'God Bless America' until everyone leaves the room. Archie gleefully finishes the entire anthem. Alone.

This episode is the embodiment of what happens when we don't listen. When we don't look for a common ground to find a new way forward. We shout each other down with our own righteous indignation. But what good comes from singing alone?

Norman Lear once said, 'This is the most emotionally cluttered era in history.' That was true back then, and some might say it's even more cluttered now. We are facing true challenges to our country, to our democracy, and to the values that many of us hold dear, such as freedom of the press and the right to protect our election process. The very idea of 'Truth' is being challenged. So how can we listen with confidence? What if we are being manipulated and fed lies? How can we cut through the clutter? How do we move to a culture of civility and dignity?

In January 2018, the US government shut down. The Republicans, who controlled both the House and Senate, and the Democrats could not agree on a new budget to keep the government open. But finally, two dozen centrist senators from both sides gathered in the office of Senator Susan Collins (Republican of Maine) to find common cause,

with the help of a Masai tribal talking stick. The stick
was a gift from Senator Heidi Heitkamp (Democrat of
North Dakota). Collins' talking stick procedure had simple
ground rules: anyone who wished to voice an opinion
could only speak once they took hold of the talking stick.
There were rumours that the stick was not always used
as intended (one rumour said it was once thrown across
Collins' office), and outside in the halls and meeting rooms
of Congress both sides were still blaming the other for
the shutdown. Collins' group, which had named itself the
Common Sense Coalition, persisted in their negotiations,
however, and within three days, they found consensus and
the government was reopened.

Voicing everyone's surprise, Senator Joe Manchin
(Democrat of West Virginia) exclaimed, 'We have basically
taken over Susan's office as our little Switzerland. That's
where we meet in a bipartisan way. Everyone talks with
each other, trying to help each other, and not at each other.'

The talking stick is not a new concept. Also called a
'Speaker's Staff', it is used by the indigenous tribes of the
Pacific Northwest. The stick is passed around a group,
from member to member, and it allows everyone to be
heard. Its presence means that only the holder can speak
while others have to listen. It gives the more introverted
members time to speak, while also keeping long-winded
individuals from dominating the discussion.

But, what happens if you do your part to listen and still
can't find 'common ground' with someone, or find yourself
utterly opposed? How do we get to the other side of
stalemate or a stand-off?

I had been touring Jerusalem, and was finally taking
a cab to Tel Aviv's Ben Gurion Airport to fly home to the
United States. The taxi driver picked me up at the hotel

for the hour-long drive. How many times have I been in a cab with an unknown driver? I didn't think of this driver as any different from the hundreds I'd had before. The man who picked me up was probably in his twenties, and he spoke fluent English. As we had a long ride to the airport, I asked him a bit about his life. He said he was Palestinian, so I asked him how it was for him living in Israel these days. For some reason, he then decided to take this opportunity to vent his rage about how the United States announced the death of Osama bin Laden. He said he didn't believe that the United States actually found and killed bin Laden, that it was all a story, like a Hollywood movie script the US government had made up in order to deceive their enemies. After all, there was no picture of his body. I interjected, saying, 'Well, it was felt that if they did, that would be seen as a desecration of Islamic burial laws.' My comment, meant to be helpful, only incensed him further. He began to get even more angry, saying that the US was a great, tyrannical evil, and that by announcing that Osama bin Laden was dead, we were just trying to brainwash the world and to, in particular, threaten the Muslim world.

I tried to speak softly so as to calm his ire: 'In spite of what you may have heard in the media, we welcome Muslims from all over the world.' But he retorted that was just another lie. I was in the back seat of his cab. There was no place for me to go. He was becoming increasingly angry. But what I was acutely aware of was that he knew that I, as an American woman, was listening to him. And all I could hope for at that moment was that I offered him the sense that he was being heard.

Of course, I thought to myself that I couldn't say for certain that Osama bin Laden had been found and killed by the Navy SEALS. I said to myself, 'Well, yes, I took it on good faith that the US government did that. I believed President Obama was telling the truth when he announced Osama Bin Laden's death on television.' But what would I gain by restating what he already knew I believed? None of us had seen the body, so we couldn't really know.

I accepted that the US government had done it, and he did not. So all I could do was listen to this very angry person, infuriated by the imperial hegemony of the United States. I felt that he was the kind of young man who needed to be persuaded that we were not all evil, but I felt the best way to do that was not by talking but by listening.

And so, all I did was *listen*. I hoped that he would notice that I wasn't arguing with him. I wasn't saying, 'You're wrong.' I looked him in the eye, as he was looking at me through the rearview mirror. I hoped that showing him these small decencies would count for something. When we finally got to the airport, he quietly and courteously pulled out my luggage, and sat it on the kerb. He stared straight at me and thanked me.

Out of respect for his culture, I knew that as a woman I should not shake his hand, and so I bowed my head and then paid and tipped him. Then, I said, 'Thank you for the ride. I wish you well.' There was the briefest hint that he was a bit ashamed that he had ranted at me for a full hour, but I felt it was far more important that he could feel the sense that he had been heard – whether I agreed with him or not. Maybe that counted for something.

My hope was that by my being open to listening to him, on this one-hour journey, perhaps a crack would appear in the solid wall of his opinion. As Leonard Cohen sang, 'There is a crack in everything. That's how the light gets in.'

Exercise: Listening requires courage

Eminent psychologist Carl Rogers said, 'If you really understand another person ... without any attempt to make evaluative judgments, you run the risk of being changed yourself. [For] the great majority of us ... listening would seem too dangerous. So the first requirement is courage.'

We all have someone in our lives with whom we think we can never find accord. We cannot bear to listen to them, or expect them to ever listen to us. But what if we could find a new way? What would it take to try and create a new path of understanding between you both?

For those seemingly impossible impasses – marital breakdown, troublesome teenagers, neighbour or family disputes – consider following these 10 steps when you come together to try and resolve the dispute:

1. Change the setting

Take yourselves apart from the usual hustle and bustle of life. Seek comfort and beauty. Instead of sitting on opposite sides of a table – as if in a divorce lawyer's conference room – find a warm, welcoming setting and seat yourselves in comfortable chairs, perhaps facing a beautiful view. You should be able to see each other but also free to let your eyes settle on a longer view. Attendees to the conflict-resolution programme known as the Oxford Process (many of whom are from the most anguished, wartorn regions of the world) are taken on a retreat, housed in beautiful Cotswold cottages, and served elegant food, the idea being that comfortable circumstances will help facilitate discussion.

2. Treat each other courteously

Offer the other person a seat and a cup of tea or coffee.

Pour it out for them. Ask about their wellbeing. Are they comfortable? What else can you do for them?

3. Seek common ground
To neutralise intense feelings, start by discussing something shared and ordinary: the weather, traffic, what movies or major sports events have happened lately. No politics!

4. Make sure both sides are allowed to speak, and be listened to, for an equal amount of time
No judgment, no interruptions, or interjections.
No righteous indignation. No visual and audible cues of disapproval. No list taking or writing anything down.

5. Paraphrase what you've heard
Once the first person has finished speaking, the other person should paraphrase what they heard. Perhaps an insight has already been gained. 'Oh, I never thought about that!' 'Oh, really, how was that?' Seek understanding.

6. Take turns
Now the other person gets the chance to speak for the same amount of time. And then the first person will paraphrase what they heard and understood. If the listener's paraphrase does not reflect what you are trying to say, the speaker can rephrase using different words and allow the listener to paraphrase again.

7. Try to understand, not judge
Both sides are free to speak their truth and their pain.
To tell their side of the story. Express your feelings. Dredge up the roots of your bitterness. Expose the wounds. Now is the time. Think back to the Native American saying, 'If you want to understand someone, walk a mile in his moccasins'.

By paraphrasing, the listening party must then reflect back how you felt, the hope being that they will begin to get a sense of how it might well have felt had they gone through those things. Carl Rogers has said that 'defensive distortions drop away with astonishing speed as people find the only intent of this experience is to understand, not to judge'.

8. Involve a third party if necessary

In certain cases you may need to include a third party. Their role will be to reflect each person's position to the other party. We can more easily understand the feelings of another person when their attitude is accurately described to us by someone else.

9. Expect there to be an Aha! moment (even if it's just a small one)

Remember: once you have seen the world the way the other person sees it – without passing any judgment – *you run the risk of being changed yourself.* This may well change your entire world – not to mention that it could upset others around you. But this is the beginning of a more understanding society.

10. Discover humility or ask for forgiveness

Dare to let go of the past, and find a new way forward.

We can all endeavour to practise this process of learning to listen well and daring to understand each other. Perhaps the real story behind these difficult times is that we are entering a new era. Some are already calling it the Age of Empathy.

I have been a seeker
and I still am.
But I stopped
asking the books
and the stars.
I started listening
to the teaching
of my soul

Rumi

Listening only
happens with time.
Take the time.
Your life will expand

9
Listen, Really Listen

Ring out, wild bells, to the wild sky ...

Ring out the old, ring in the new ...
Ring out the false, ring in the true ...

Ring out the want, the care, the sin,
The faithless coldness of the times ...

Ring out false pride in place and blood,
The civic slander and the spite;
Ring in the love of truth and right,
Ring in the common love of good.

Alfred, Lord Tennyson, *In Memoriam CVI* (Abridged)

When I was a student at Northwestern University near Chicago, I was extremely fortunate to study under the ground-breaking Professor of Speech and Performance Arts, Charlotte I. Lee, whose mantra was, 'Listen, *really listen* to the words.' She taught us to apply the concept of kinaesthesia to language – proposing that all language creates a visceral connection with our feelings and senses, and embeds within us like muscle memory. This is the true power of great poetry and prose. We read John Ciardi's *How Does A Poem Mean*, which instructed us not just to read poetry, but to read it *aloud*, so that we could feel the poet's intention through not only the word choices, but through rhythm and cadence. This is yet another way we enlarge our imaginations and cultivate wonder. Reading aloud is a shared experience. One speaks, the other listens.

In each class with Professor Lee, we read aloud from the great poets – as many as we could. We read everything from the great lamentation of Shakespeare's King Lear (*'Never, never, never, never, never'*), to John Keats (*'Beauty is truth, truth beauty – that is all Ye know on earth, and all ye need to know'*) to Dylan Thomas (*'Do not go gentle into that good night, Rage, rage against the dying of the light'*) to E.E. Cummings (*'anyone lived in a pretty how town'*) to Emily Dickinson (*'Because I could not stop for Death, He kindly stopped for me'*).

There were many others – far too many to list here – but after each class, we all came away almost levitating. I was quite simply inspired in a way no other course I've ever taken has inspired me, and I think it was because we had listened to and shared the realms of great minds *out loud*.

The great poets gave me 'ears to hear'. I learned to listen to how they built their ideas with the musicality of language, cadence, rhyme structure, and how all of that comes together in elegant precision in order to create the poem's full intent.

In the Tennyson poem quoted at the beginning of this chapter, he masterfully creates the sound and feeling of bells ringing wildly. In the first line, 'Ring out, wild bells, to the wild sky,' twice the word *wild* uplifts, as if the up-and-down forces of the bells are catapulting the bell higher and higher. Each subsequent line sounds and feels like the to and fro of church bells in riotous joy, until the very last line of the verses reproduced here: 'Ring in the common love of good.' Then the cadence slows down as if the bell ringer is letting go of each pull, and the bell slows to a halt.

As I mentioned earlier in this book, my favourite sound memory from my childhood was the closing *thwack* of a porch screen door on a hot summer's evening. Once the latch shut, it meant you were in for the night. But then, came the advent of air conditioning and double-glazed glass, and that sound went away with my childhood. Somehow it haunted me, though. I knew that sound was unique to that time and place in my childhood.

A couple of years ago, I took a week's retreat at the Abbey of Gethsemani in Bardstown, Kentucky – famously the spiritual home of poet, social activist and prolific author Thomas Merton. In the mid-nineteenth century, French Trappist Monks had bought two thousand acres of Kentucky woodlands and built their monastery during the Civil War years. Merton converted to Catholicism in the 1930s and entered the abbey in 1941, where he was ordained as Father Louis.

During the week, we were all obliged to go about our daily life in silence. A friend of mine arranged a meeting between myself and Brother Paul – who had been a novice under Merton – and we met in a side office where we were free to talk. Brother Paul asked me if I would like to visit Merton's hermitage where he had lived on the outskirts of the Abbey's woodlands in the last years of his life. I was deeply honoured, and said, 'Of course, I would love to.' We drove down a dusty country lane, far into the woods, until we came upon a very humble two-room cement-block home with a simple front porch. Inside, set before a wide window looking out on a clearing in the forest, sat Merton's desk where he wrote, prayed and meditated. In the centre of the room stood a wood-burning stove, and along the walls were shelves filled with Merton's diaries. The second room was a primitive kitchen with a hot plate and a simple bed. Off to the side was Merton's own chapel where he took the daily Eucharist. I was deeply moved that I could sit at his desk and look out at his view, which I imagined had remained relatively unchanged since his passing in 1968, while on a trip to Bangkok to appeal for interfaith understanding between Buddhists and Christians. Very few people were given this opportunity to be here.

Then we walked out the front screen door and *I heard it.* A subtle screech, the *thwack.* Merton's screen door. I waited for it to close. Brother Paul asked me why I was staring at it. I told him how I was astonished to hear this childhood memory come alive. He said, 'Well, that screen door was here when Merton was, no doubt about it. He would have heard it, too.'

Each sound – like a snowflake – is unique. Sound waves are living; they only exist in time as it's passing. The knowledge that that particular sound had been heard daily by Merton made me feel that somehow we were connected.

So far I have put a lot of emphasis on sound, but where does this connect with people who are deaf or hard of hearing? I have met with several vibrant actors from the Tony-nominated Deaf West Theatre in Los Angeles, and they spoke with disdain of the 'hearing world's' belief that all deaf people want cochlear implants that would allow them to experience the world of audible sound. I'll bet many of us have watched and wept happily at the YouTube videos of the moving, teary reactions of formerly deaf people hearing for the very first time once the cochlear implant is turned on, and although there is no doubt that this is an electrifying, mind-blowing experience for those who elect to have the procedure, the deaf actors I met say that they themselves 'hear' just fine – because they 'listen' with full attention to each other. They connect and thrive as deaf people, and they love the beauty and expressiveness of signing. One thing I noticed being in a room full of deaf individuals passionately signing is that they are fully focused on each other – looking, observing and reacting. They take each other in with kindness and courtesy. In fact, I felt like the outsider that I was, sure that I was missing out on their great camaraderie.

Dame Evelyn Glennie, the Scottish virtuoso percussionist, became profoundly deaf at the age of twelve and thereafter taught herself to hear with parts of her body other than her ears. In her 2003 TED talk, 'How to Truly Listen' she said, 'My aim really is to teach the world to listen. That's my only real aim in life.' She now performs worldwide, saying, 'We're all connected by sound.' When she lost her hearing, she was fortunate to find a music teacher who could teach her to listen through her body. She mastered a range of percussion instruments – including the xylophone, snare drum, timpani, and even the Great Highland bagpipes – by, first of all, taking off her shoes and listening through her bare feet, using vibrations to interpret the sound.

She became accomplished through years of practice, and yet when she applied to the Royal Academy of Music in London, she was roundly dismissed. They told her that they could not support her because they knew of no career she could have as a deaf musician. But Glennie and her family prevailed in the end – appealing for her admission on the terms that every entrant *had the right to be heard*, and accepted or rejected based on their musical ability alone. After her second audition, she was accepted, and the academy opened its doors to people with disabilities of all types. Today Evelyn has an illustrious career, which includes performing solo concerts and with orchestras all over the world. Indeed, she made a dramatic entrance at the opening ceremony of the London 2012 Olympic Games when she led one thousand drummers into the arena.

Evelyn Glennie's success has furthered the cause of inclusivity and opened the doors for others coming after her, but she is still what we would call an 'outlier'. She is not typical; she has pushed the envelope and done extraordinary things.

Yet it is the derring-do of society's outliers that has helped civilisation advance. Outliers are the visionary thinkers, artists, rebels and adventurers who seek out new realms. The outliers dare others to listen to their point of view – which, of course, can feel threatening *because it's a new idea.*

Since time immemorial, it was the outlier who made the decision to leave their own tribe, traipse through wild, uncharted territory and venture into foreign enclaves. Imagine how that group felt when they saw this stranger. If they killed him, well, the story is over. But when the hosts and the newcomer dared to meet around the campfire and listen – they would invariably find new common ground, even if they didn't know each other's language. The outlier would show them, perhaps, his sack full of berries: 'Hey, we found a use for these berries. Try this.' Or draw in the mud: 'There's a great plain two valleys away full of game and wild boars.' Or demonstrate: 'We learned how to heal this illness by using this poultice.'

> Never question the wisdom of what you fail to understand, for the world is filled with wonders.

L. Frank Baum, *The Wonderful World of Oz*

Listening is to wonder, what breathing is to life. To listen well, you open yourself to the other person, you give them your attention and your time. You are taken on a journey. And if you've listened well, you're never quite the same again. Your life horizons will expand.

To thrive we must cultivate wonder. When we despair, grow cynical and snarky, and self-select our own filter bubbles, we diminish our capacity. We become smug, self-satisfied know-it-alls; 'been there, done that'.

Perhaps the hardest thing to do as we grow up and grow older is to stay young and curious. Cultivating wonder is as essential to our wellbeing as eating well, exercising and loving well.

In his 1992 book of daily meditations, *Listening to Your Life*, Presbyterian minister and Pulitzer Prize finalist Frederick Buechner tells the story of a great theologian who was lecturing at length on the subject of miracles. When he was challenged to name one miracle he had personally experienced, he replied, 'There is only one miracle. It is life.' Buechner goes on to ask readers the following questions:

Have you wept at anything during the past year?
Has your heart beat faster at the sight of young beauty?
Have you thought seriously about the fact that someday you are going to die?

More often than not, do you really listen when people are speaking to you instead of just waiting for your time to speak?

One young woman had similar advice to share. Holly Butcher, a 27-year-old from New South Wales, Australia, died on 4 January 2018 from Ewing's sarcoma, a rare form of bone cancer. Among many wise offerings from those who have been given the gift of knowing their days are numbered, she left behind an open letter to the world which she asked her family to post on Facebook after her death. In it, she says:

> Get up early sometimes and listen to the birds while you watch the beautiful colours the sun makes as it rises. Listen to music. Really listen. Music is therapy. Old is best. Talk to your friends. Put down your phone. Are they doing okay? Tell your loved ones you love them every time you get the chance and love them with everything you have.

In the course of writing this book, I've been repeatedly struck by the fact that the word *listen* is often the last word in a sentence – a kind of final surrender or a noble bow. And there *is* something noble about it. Somehow, by listening and not returning fire with fire, we move on to a kinder and more mature place of understanding. Such is the power of listening well: we experience truth. And we flourish for it – our hearts expand, our minds burst open – creating one fleeting touchpoint in our briefly crossing orbits.

Listening only occurs in time. Take the time. Each moment we listen creates a common good. Let us all do this one good thing: Listen.

Being heard is so close
to being loved that for
the average person,
they are almost
indistinguishable

—

David Augsburger

Resources

Watch

Films
Here is a selection of films
with masterful sound design.

2001: A Space Odyssey,
dir. Stanley Kubrick

American Graffiti
dir. George Lucas
sound by Walter Murch

Apocalypse Now
dir. Francis Ford Coppola
sound by Walter Murch

The Birds
dir. Alfred Hitchcock

Blade Runner
dir. Ridley Scott

Blue Velvet
dir. David Lynch
sound by Alan Splet

Braveheart
dir. Mel Gibson
sound by Anna Behlmer

Breathless
dir. Jean-Luc Godard

Citizen Kane
dir. Orson Welles

A Clockwork Orange
dir. Stanley Kubrick

The Conversation
dir. Francis Ford Coppola
sound by Walter Murch

The Elephant Man
dir. David Lynch
sound by Alan Splet

Eraserhead
dir. David Lynch
sound by Alan Splet

ET
dir. Steven Spielberg
sound by Ben Burtt

Finding Nemo
dir. Andrew Stanton
sound by Gary Rydstrom

Gladiator
dir. Ridley Scott
sound by Karen Baker
Landers and Per Hallberg

The Godfather & Godfather II
dir. Francis Ford Coppola
sound by Walter Murch

Gravity
dir. Alfonso Cuarón
sound by Glenn Freemantle

Inside Out
dir. Pete Docter
sound by Ren Klyce

Jurassic Park
dir. Steven Spielberg
sound by Gary Rydstrom

Lincoln
dir. Steven Spielberg
sound by Gary Rydstrom
and Ben Burtt

Luxo Jr.
dir. John Lasseter
sound by Gary Rydstrom and
Ben Burtt

Mad Max Fury Road
dir. George Miller
sound by Mark Mangini

Ordinary People
dir. Robert Redford
sound by Kay Rose

Raging Bull
dir. Martin Scorsese
sound by Frank Warner

Rear Window
dir. Alfred Hitchcock

A River Runs Through It
dir. Robert Redford
sound by Gary Rydstrom

Saving Private Ryan
dir. Steven Spielberg
sound by Gary Rydstrom

Schindler's List
dir. Steven Spielberg

The Social Network
dir. David Fincher
sound by Ren Klyce

Spartacus
dir. Stanley Kubrick

A Star is Born
dir. Frank Pierson
(sound overseen by
Barbra Streisand)

Star Wars Episodes IV, V & VI
dir. George Lucas
sound by Ben Burtt

Toy Story 1, 2 & 3
dir. John Lasseter
sound by Gary Rydstrom

Tin Toy
dir. John Lasseter
sound by Gary Rydstrom

Trainspotting
dir. Danny Boyle

Up
dir. Pete Docter
sound by Tom Myers

Wall-E
dir. Andrew Stanton
sound by Ben Burtt

Documentaries
Alive Inside: A Story of Music and Memory
dir. Michael Rossato-Bennett (2014), Netflix

The Art of Listening
dir. Michael Coleman & Emmanuel Moran (2017)
theartoflisteningfilm.com

Making Waves: The Art of Cinematic Sound
dir. Midge Costin (2018)

Listen

Radio
Across the Red Line
BBC Radio Four

Talks
ted.com

Evelyn Glennie, 'How To Truly Listen'

Bernie Krause, 'The Voice of The Natural World'

Julian Treasure (various)

Read

Books
The Great Animal Orchestra: Finding the Origins of Music in the World's Wild Places
Bernie Krause

Seven Thousand Ways to Listen: Staying Close to What Is Sacred
Mark Nepo

A Listening Ear
Paul Tournier

On Becoming a Person: A Therapist's View of Psychotherapy
Carl R. Rogers

Listening to Your Life:
Daily Meditations
Frederick Buechner

Articles

Psychology Today
The Key to Intimacy is Radical
Listening by Nancy Colier

TheGuardian.com
The 10 best recordings of
poets (including Alfred,
Lord Tennyson, W.H. Auden,
Sylvia Plath, Philip Larkin
and Alice Oswald)

Smithsonianmag.com
Marian Anderson singing
at the Lincoln Memorial,
9 April 1939

About the Author

Bobette Buster is the author of *Do Story: How to Tell Your Story so the World Listens* (Do Books 2013); the writer and producer of feature documentary, *Making Waves: The Art of Cinematic Sound* (2018) and several feature and documentary projects, including *Charlotte* and *Laughing Matters: How Satire Shaped American Culture*. In 2019, she gave a TEDx Lecture entitled, *The Radical Act of Storytelling*.

She has been a story consultant and speaker to major studios including Pixar, Disney, Sony Animation and Amazon Games, and to leading production companies, as well as advertising and marketing agencies around the world.

She lectures and serves on the visiting faculties of academic institutions, most recently as the Professor of the Practice of Digital Storytelling at Northeastern University and Adjunct Professor of Storytelling and Science Communication at Tufts University.

She lives in Los Angeles, California.

You can connect with Bobette on social media: *@bobettebuster* or via her website: *bobettebuster.com*

Thanks

To the students and participants in all my story classes worldwide, you taught me the joy of listening. I have flourished, and am far better for having heard your stories.

To all my friends around the world – the tall ships, stable and able, in their journeys – Armando Fumagalli, Brian Eastman and Christabel Alberry, David and Clare Hieatt and the Do community. To the friends who define longevity and constancy: M'Leigh Koziol, Chuck Slocum, Karen Johnson, Gwen Terpstra and Mary Cellini. My beloved brother, Eric, my aunt, Margie, and my cousins Mark and Rachelle, Madison, Morgan, Gianna, Philip, Joseph and Robbie. And my wonderful support, Jody Berges.

To my editor and publisher Miranda West – spitfire, very definition of 'command', a general among us. Thank you for listening to what others have said about my workshops and lectures, and asking me to fulfil this great task.

Index

Notes

Books in the series

Do Agile Tim Drake

Do Beekeeping Orren Fox

Do Birth Caroline Flint

Do Breathe
　　　Michael Townsend Williams

Do Build Alan Moore

Do Death Amanda Blainey

Do Design Alan Moore

Do Disrupt Mark Shayler

Do Earth Tamsin Omond

Do Fly Gavin Strange

Do Grow Alice Holden

Do Improvise Robert Poynton

Do Inhabit Sue Fan, Danielle Quigley

Do Lead Les McKeown

Do Listen Bobette Buster

Do Make James Otter

Do Open David Hieatt

Do Pause Robert Poynton

Do Photo Andrew Paynter

Do Present Mark Shayler

Do Preserve
　　　Anja Dunk, Jen Goss, Mimi Beaven

Do Protect Johnathan Rees

Do Purpose David Hieatt

Do Scale Les McKeown

Do Sea Salt
　　　Alison, David & Jess Lea-Wilson

Do Sing James Sills

Do Sourdough Andrew Whitley

Do Story Bobette Buster

Do Team Charlie Gladstone

Do Walk Libby DeLana

Do Wild Baking Tom Herbert

Also available

Path A short story about reciprocity Louisa Thomsen Brits

The Skimming Stone A short story about courage Dominic Wilcox

Stay Curious How we created a world class event in a cowshed Clare Hieatt

The Path of a Doer A simple tale of how to get things done David Hieatt

Available in print, digital and audio formats from booksellers or via our website: **thedobook.co**

To hear about events and forthcoming titles, you can find us on social media @dobookco, or subscribe to our newsletter